CRYSTAL ANGEL

AFFIRMATIONS

BRENDA DEHAAN

DeHaan, Brenda
Crystal Angel Affirmations

1. Angels. 2. Affirmations. 3. Mind-Body-Spirit.
4. Gemstones. 5. Rocks and minerals. 6.
Inspiration.
7. Self-help.

Summary: Carved gemstone angels are photographed in an array of settings. Each one has an affirmation for personal positive thinking.

Contents

~*~ Angels and Affirmations ~*~ 4

~*~ Amethyst ~*~.. 5

~*~ Angelite ~*~ 6

~*~ Black Agate ~*~ 7

~*~ Black Tourmaline ~*~ 8

~*~ Blue Goldstone ~*~ 9

~*~ Calcite ~*~ 10

~*~ Clear Quartz ~*~ 11

~*~ Goldstone ~*~ 12

~*~ Green Aventurine ~*~ 13

~*~ Indigo Gabbro ~*~.. 14

~*~ Labradorite ~*~ 15

~*~ Lapis Lazuli ~*~ 16

~*~ Moss Agate ~*~ 17

~*~ Pyrite ~*~ 18

~*~ Rainbow ~*~ 19

~*~ Red Aventurine ~*~ 20

~*~ Rose Quartz ~*~ 21

~*~ Snow Quartz ~*~ 22

~*~ Sodalite ~*~ 23

~*~ Sunstone ~*~ 24

~*~ Tiger's Eye ~*~ 25

~*~ Unakite ~*~ 26

~*~ Vessonite ~*~ 27

~*~ Yellow Quartz ~*~ 28

~*~ I AM ~*~ 29

~*~ Angels and Affirmations ~*~

People are comforted when envisioning angels watching over them. Carved gemstone angels are tangible reminders that also bring comfort, inspiration, and healing.

Affirmations are reminders to believe the *best* in yourself. They help you to visualize the possibilities right in front of you.

Combine angels and affirmations for double the comfort, double the positivity, double the inspiration.

The creative settings make each affirmation more memorable. The angels and affirmations may differ in their personal significance, depending on your life's current situation. They each help the future to look better than ever.

Affirmations are an uplifting way to start and end your day. Believe and achieve!

~*~ Amethyst ~*~

I am intuitive and compelling.

~*~ Angelite ~*~

I am blessed by angels on earth,

angels above...angels all around.

~*~ Black Agate ~*~

I am grounded and balanced.

~*~ **Black Tourmaline** ~*~

**I am surrounded with
calming protection.**

~*~ Blue Goldstone ~*~

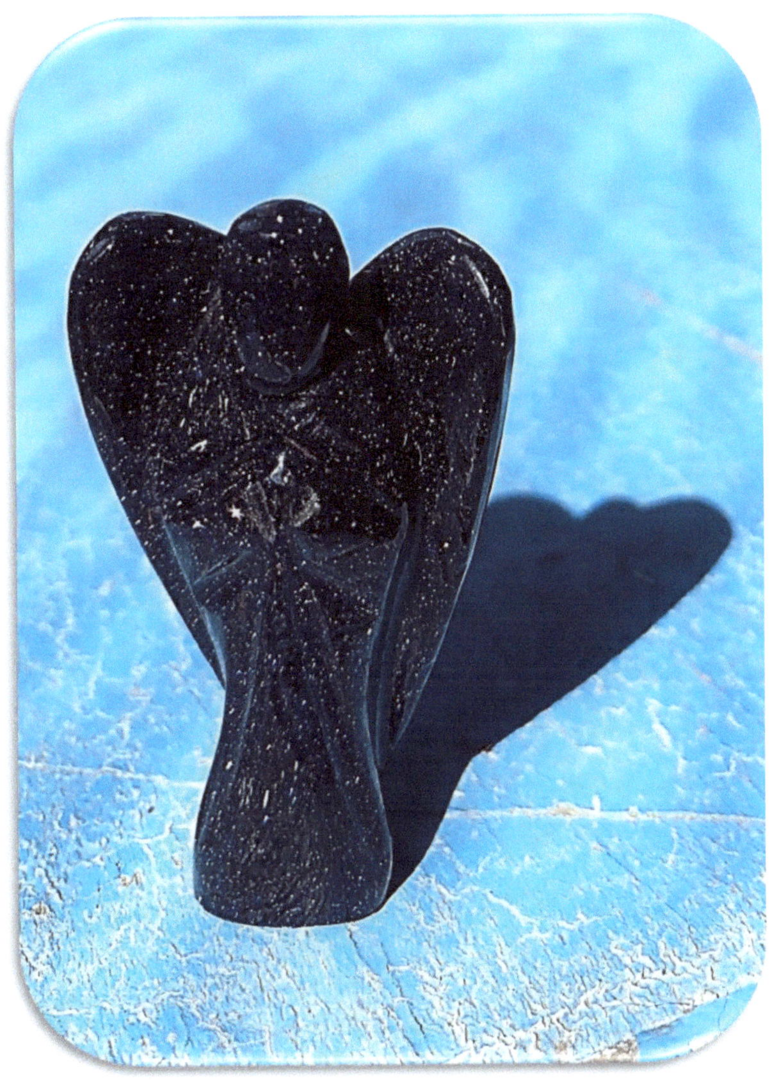

**I am sparking with confidence
and vitality.**

~*~ Calcite ~*~

I am a student of life.

~*~ Clear Quartz ~*~

I am a master of many things.

~*~ Goldstone ~*~

I am ambitious and ingenious.

~*~ Green Aventurine ~*~

I am healing in harmony.

~*~ Indigo Gabbro ~*~

I am independent, unified,
and whole.

~*~ Labradorite ~*~

I am incredible, imaginative, and
aware of transformations.

~*~ Lapis Lazuli ~*~

I am beautiful, peaceful,

and truthful.

~*~ Moss Agate ~*~

**I am creative, rational,
growing and grounded.**

I am perceptive and prosperous.

I am colorful and complete.

I am enthusiastic and determined.

I am loveable and loving,

forgiving, and serene.

~*~ Snow Quartz ~*~

**I am pure and innocent,
marveling at life.**

~*~ Sodalite ~*~

I am calm, understanding, and true.

**I am joyously radiant,
shining year round.**

~*~ Tiger's Eye ~*~

I am worthy, courageous,
and insightful.

**I am compassionate, nurturing,
and kind.**

~*~ Vessonite ~*~

I am inventive, organized, supportive, and loyal.

~*~ Yellow Quartz ~*~

**I am creative and cheerful,
optimistic and open-minded.**

I am what I need to be.
I am what I want to be.
I am.

About the Author

*This book was first released in honor of
my mom's milestone birthday.
Angelic blessings to you, Patricia Boughey!
You are an angel on earth, and I love you very much!*

Brenda DeHaan is the author of an eclectic mix of books that reflect her interests: writing, library genrefication, healing crystals, children's picture books, craft fairs, young adult self-help, and hospitality.

Crystal Angel Affirmations was translated into German by Gesine Reinhold, ***Wie Kristallengel ermutigen,*** and into Spanish by Erin Knudsen, ***Las afirmaciones con los Ángeles de Piedras Preciosas.***

Books by Brenda DeHaan

Healing crystals
*Crystal Angel Affirmations (also in Spanish and German)
*Crystal Haiku: Nature Poetry That ROCKS!
*Rockin' Crystals: How Healing Crystals Can Rock Your Life
*My Amethyst Journal
*My Rose Quartz Journal
*My Apache Tear Journal

Crafting
*Craft Fairs from A to Z
*29 Tips for Craft Fair Vendors
Jewelry Vendors' Guidebook
*Host a Successful Craft Fair
*The Craft Fair Vendor Guidebook: Ideas to Inspire
*Crafty Decluttering

Children's books
*ABC Amazing Book of Crystals
*Rocks Rock: Rough and Tumbled, Colorful and Cool
From Apple to Zombie: Illustrate Your Own Halloween Book
*Cat Naps, Dog Naps: Who Naps More?
*Adventures with Apollo: The Cat Who Rules Rooftops
*The Flower Fairies Meet the Talking Rainbow Rocks
*Beach Surprise: Unicorns, Mermaids, Flower Fairies, and
Rainbow Rocks Meet at the Beach
*Crystals for Kids: Learn the Names of 17 Rocks & Minerals
*Rocks with Socks and Fox
*Rocks and Rhyme 2 in One Fun
*Hooray for a Fun Day! A Small Town Celebration

Tween and Teens
*Life Advice for Teens from an Ageless Grandma
*Shine Like a Crystal: 12 Quick tips to Rock Life

Writing
*Self-Publishing Painlessly for Free

Library genrefication
*Where Are the Spooky Books? How to Genrefy Your Library